YOU CAN TEACH YOURSELF® ACCORDION

by Neil Griffin

Photos courtesy of Hohner and Castiglione

CD Contents

1. Learning the C's (:19)
2. Putting the C's Together (:54)
3. Adding the G's (:16)
4. Mixing the C's and G's (:48)
5. Adding D, E, and F (:20)
6. Put it All Together (:48)
7. Bass and Chord Rhythm Drill (1:07)
8. Oom-Pah-Pah Waltz (:37)
9. Everybody Has Their Ups and Downs (:35)
10. New G Hand Position (:27)
11. Déja Vu in G (:34)
12. Children's Song (:44)
13. Learning Eighth Notes (:32)
14. Minuet (1:06)
15. Ode to Joy (:55)
16. Air (:39)
17. Gavotte (1:38)
18. The British Grenadiers (:36)
19. Alternating the Bass Notes (:31)
20. Amazing Grace (:39)
21. Key Signatures (1:03)
22. Lullaby (:32)
23. Introducing the Minor Chords (:30)
24. Hungarian Dance #4 (:46)
25. Introducing the 7th Chords (:31)
26. The God of Abraham Praise (:49)
27. Skaters Waltz (:31)
28. French Song (:52)
29. Sur le Pont d'Avignon (:51)
30. Wandering (:30)
31. The Bells of St. Marys (:52)
32. Polka, Polka (1:02)
33. Are You from Dixie (:57)
34. Lake Charles Waltz (1:03)
35. 6/8 Time (:26)
36. When Johnny Comes Marching Home (:39)
37. Come Back to Sorrento (1:31)
38. Two Steppin' 'Cross Texas (1:05)
39. Julida Polka (:31)
40. Andante (1:06)
41. Jambalaya (1:07)
42. Pretty Fair Maid Jig (1:33)
43. Peg o' My Heart (:44)
44. Rattle the Bottles Reel (:48)
45. Rick's Reel (:49)
46. Introducing the Counter-Bass Notes (:17)
47. Counter-Bass Notes-2 (:14)
48. Counter-Bass Notes-3 (:55)
49. March (1:30)
50. Introducing the Diminished Chords (:26)
51. Ja-da (:40)
52. Chinatown (1:02)
53. I Want a Girl, Just Like the Girl (1:08)
54. I Love You Truly (:59)
55. Smiles (1:06)
56. For Me and My Gal (1:05)
57. Washington and Lee Swing (1:01)
58. Fascination (1:10)
59. El Capitan March (1:15)
60. Sweetheart of Sigma Chi (1:11)
61. Melancholy Baby (1:20)
62. El Caballo Bayo (1:50)
63. Mexican Siesta (1:16)

1 2 3 4 5 6 7 8 9 0

© 1997 BY MEL BAY PUBLICATIONS, INC., PACIFIC, MO 63069.
ALL RIGHTS RESERVED. INTERNATIONAL COPYRIGHT SECURED. B.M.I. MADE AND PRINTED IN U.S.A.

Visit us on the Web at http://www.melbay.com — E-mail us at email@melbay.com

CONTENTS

Parts of the Accordion 3	*French Song* 43
About the Accordion 3	*Sur le Pont d'Avignon* 44
Holding the Accordion 4	*Wandering* 45
Reference Section 5	*The Bells of St. Marys* 46
The Left Hand 9	Sixteenth Notes 47
The Right Hand 11	Eighth Rest 47
Learning the C's 13	*Polka, Polka* 47
Adding the G's 15	*Are You from Dixie* 48
Proper Use of the Bellows 16	Grace Notes 50
The Tie 18	*Lake Charles Waltz* 50
Bass and Chord Rhythm Drill 19	6/8 Time 52
Oom-Pah-Pah Waltz 20	*When Johnny Comes Marching Home* 53
Everybody Has Their Ups and Down 21	*Come Back to Sorrento* 54
New G Hand Position 22	Dotted Eighths and Sixteenths 56
Déja Vu in G 23	*Two Steppin' 'Cross Texas* 56
Repeat Sign 24	*Julida Polka* 58
D.C. al Fine 24	Staccato 59
Children's Song 24	Legato 59
Notes and Rests 25	Andante 59
Learning Eighth Notes 25	*Jambalaya* 60
Minuet 26	*Pretty Fair Maid Jig* 62
Dotted Quarter Note 27	*Peg o' My Heart* 63
Ode to Joy 27	*Rattle the Bottles Reel* 64
The Slur 28	*Rick's Reel* 65
Air 28	Introducing the Counter-Bass Notes 66
New C Hand Position 29	*March* 69
Gavotte 29	Introducing the Diminished Chords 70
The British Grenadiers 30	*Ja-da* 71
Alternating the Bass Notes 31	*Chinatown* 72
The Triplet 32	*I Want a Girl, Just Like the Girl* 74
Amazing Grace 32	*I Love You Truly* 76
Chromatics 33	*Smiles* 78
Flats 34	*For Me and My Gal* 80
Naturals 34	*Washington and Lee Swing* 82
Key Signatures 35	*Fascination* 84
Sustained Bass Notes 36	*El Capitan March* 86
Lullaby 36	*Sweetheart of Sigma Chi* 88
Introducing the Minor Chords 37	*Melancholy Baby* 90
Relative Minor Keys 38	Right-Hand Harmony 92
Hungarian Dance #4 39	*El Caballo Bayo* 92
Introducing the 7th Chords 40	*Mexican Siesta* 94
The God of Abraham Praise 41	Bass and Chord Button Review 96
Skaters Waltz 42	

PARTS OF THE ACCORDION

ABOUT THE ACCORDION

The accordion is one of the world's most complete musical instruments. Why? Because it provides all the main ingredients — bass, harmony, and melody — all at the same time.

Although a little extra coordination is required, the accordion is probably one of the easiest musical instruments to learn to play. It is, of course, the predecessor of the chord organ and the electric keyboards that are so popular today.

The accordion is a "personal" type of instrument which continues to be enjoyed by thousands of people of widely varied ethnic origins. Think about it — French Canadian, Cajun, Tex-Mex, Irish, German, Italian, Spanish, Polish, etc., etc., etc.…

When the batteries run down or electricity is not readily available, or everyone begins to tire of all the synthetically produced music…

PICK UP YOUR ACCORDION AND "SMILE."

HOLDING THE ACCORDION

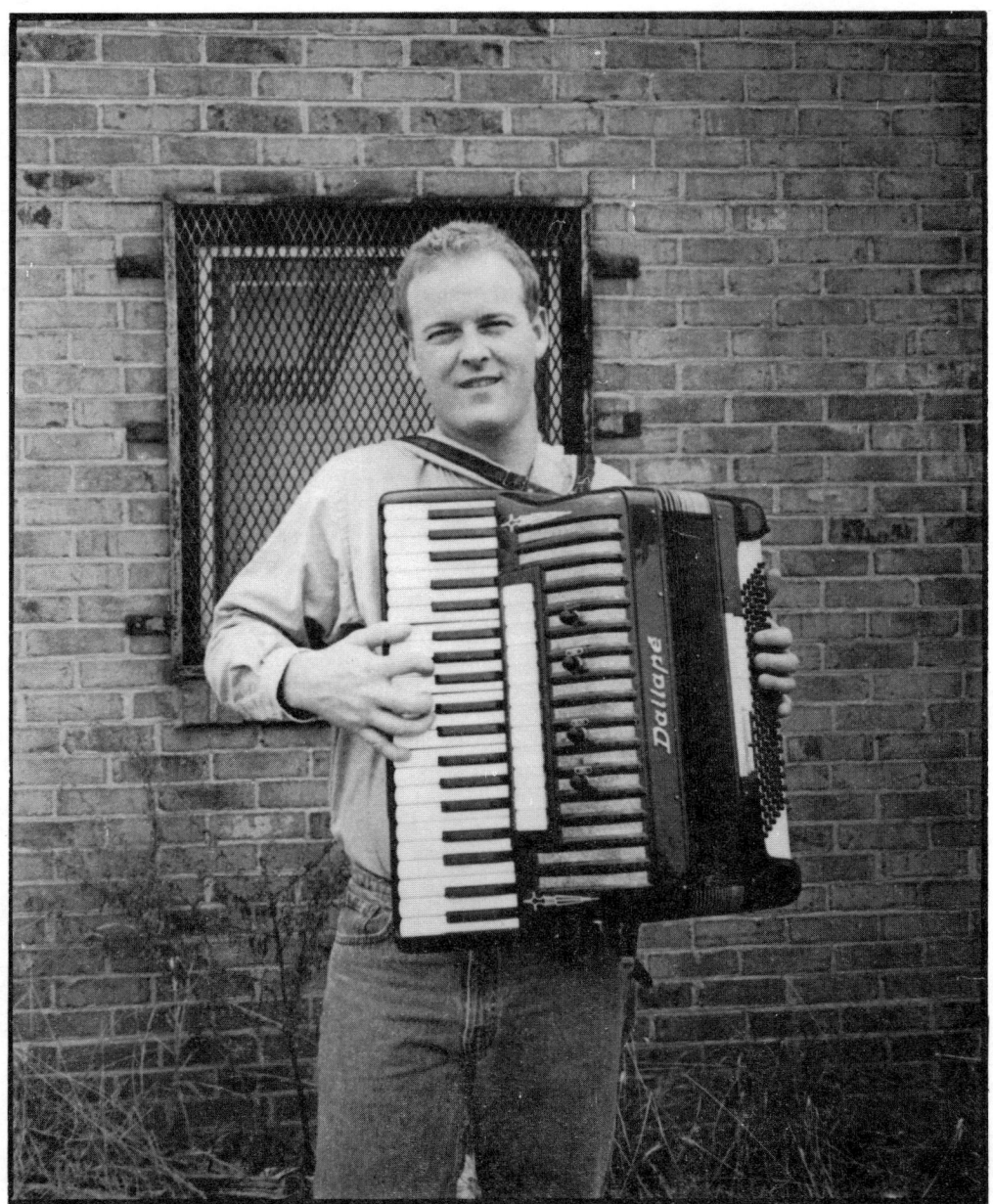

HOLDING THE ACCORDION CORRECTLY – WHETHER STANDING OR SITTING AFFECTS BOTH APPEARANCE AND PERFORMANCE.

NOTICE THE FOLLOWING IMPORTANT POINTS DEMONSTRATED IN THE ABOVE PHOTO.

THE KEYBOARD IS ONLY A FEW INCHES BELOW THE CHIN.

THE BLACK KEYS ARE DIRECTLY IN LINE UNDER THE CHIN
AND VERTICAL WITH THE CENTER LINE OF THE BODY.

THE BACK STRAPS ARE ADJUSTED TIGHTLY, PREVENTING THE ACCORDION FROM
MOVING SIDE TO SIDE WHEN THE BELLOWS ARE OPENED AND CLOSED.

REFERENCE SECTION

So that you will have a central place to refer to concerning musical information and specific explanations about mechanical as well as musical aspects of the accordion — several pages of illustrations and/or charts are included at this point.

Don't try to memorize all of this — just read through it and, as you proceed through this "Teach Yourself Method," it will be available to help you at any time.

Grey shaded boxes will appear throughout this book explaining and/or illustrating each new item as it is needed to play the next tune(s) correctly.

You are strongly advised to use this material in the order it is presented. Of course, a qualified teacher is helpful if available in your area.

HERE WE GO!

120-Bass Accordion

Notes

This is a note: 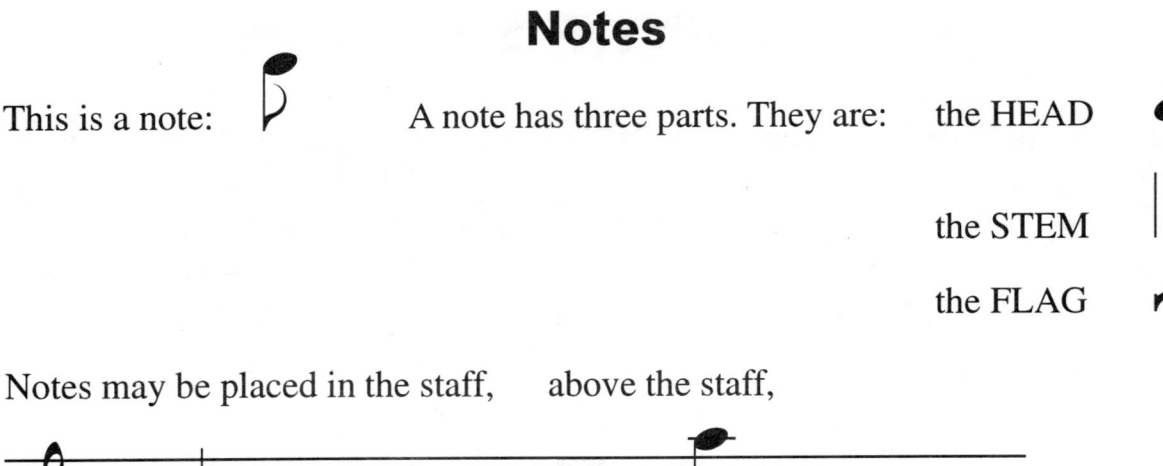   A note has three parts. They are: the HEAD

the STEM

the FLAG

Notes may be placed in the staff,   above the staff,

and below the staff.

A note will bear the name of the line or space it occupies on the staff.
The location of a note in, above, or below the staff will indicate the pitch.

PITCH: The height or depth of a tone.   **TONE:** A musical sound.

Types of Notes

The type of note will indicate the length of its sound:

𝅝	This is a whole note. The head is hollow. It does not have a stem.	𝅝	= four beats A whole note will receive four beats or counts.
𝅗𝅥	This is a half note. The head is hollow. It has a stem.	𝅗𝅥	= two beats A half note will receive two beats or counts.
𝅘𝅥	This is a quarter note. The head is solid. It has a stem.	𝅘𝅥	= one beat A quarter note will receive one beat or count.
𝅘𝅥𝅮	This is an eighth note. The head is solid. It has a stem and a flag.	𝅘𝅥𝅮	= a half beat An eighth note will receive a half beat or count (two for one beat).

Rests

A REST is a sign used to designate a period of silence. This period of silence will be of the same duration of time as the note to which it corresponds.

𝄾 This is an eighth rest.   𝄽 This is a quarter rest.

▬ This is a half rest. Notice that is lies on the line.

▬ This is a whole rest. Notice that is hangs down from the line. In 3/4 time it also serves as a whole-measure rest.

NOTES

WHOLE	HALF	QUARTER	EIGHTH
4 COUNTS	2 COUNTS	1 COUNT	2 FOR 1 COUNT

RESTS

48-Bass Accordion

The Time Signature

The above examples are the common types of time signatures to be used in this book.

$\frac{4}{4}$ The top number indicates the number of beats per measure.

$\frac{4}{4}$ The bottom number indicates the type of note receiving one beat per measure.

$\frac{4}{4}$ 4 beats per measure. A quarter note receives one beat.

$\frac{6}{8}$ 6 beats per measure. Each eighth note receives one full beat.

 Signifies so-called "common time" and is simply another way of designating 4/4 time.

8

THE LEFT HAND

The left side of the accordion (the side with all the buttons) consists of two types of buttons that produce two types of sounds:

1. BASS BUTTONS that sound only single bass tones which provide standard bass parts, short bass runs, and even bass solos.

2. CHORD BUTTONS that sound several tones at the same time and provide the accompaniment harmony.

On the 120 bass accordion, which is considered the standard accordion, there are 20 diagonal rows. Each of these rows contains 6 buttons. LEARN THESE BUTTONS WELL, as every one of the 20 rows has the same layout, and only the musical pitches change from row to row.

Shown below is the "C" row, generally considered as home-base from which you learn to feel your way to the other rows. The regular "C" bass button will either have a dip or jewel so that you can find it by feel.

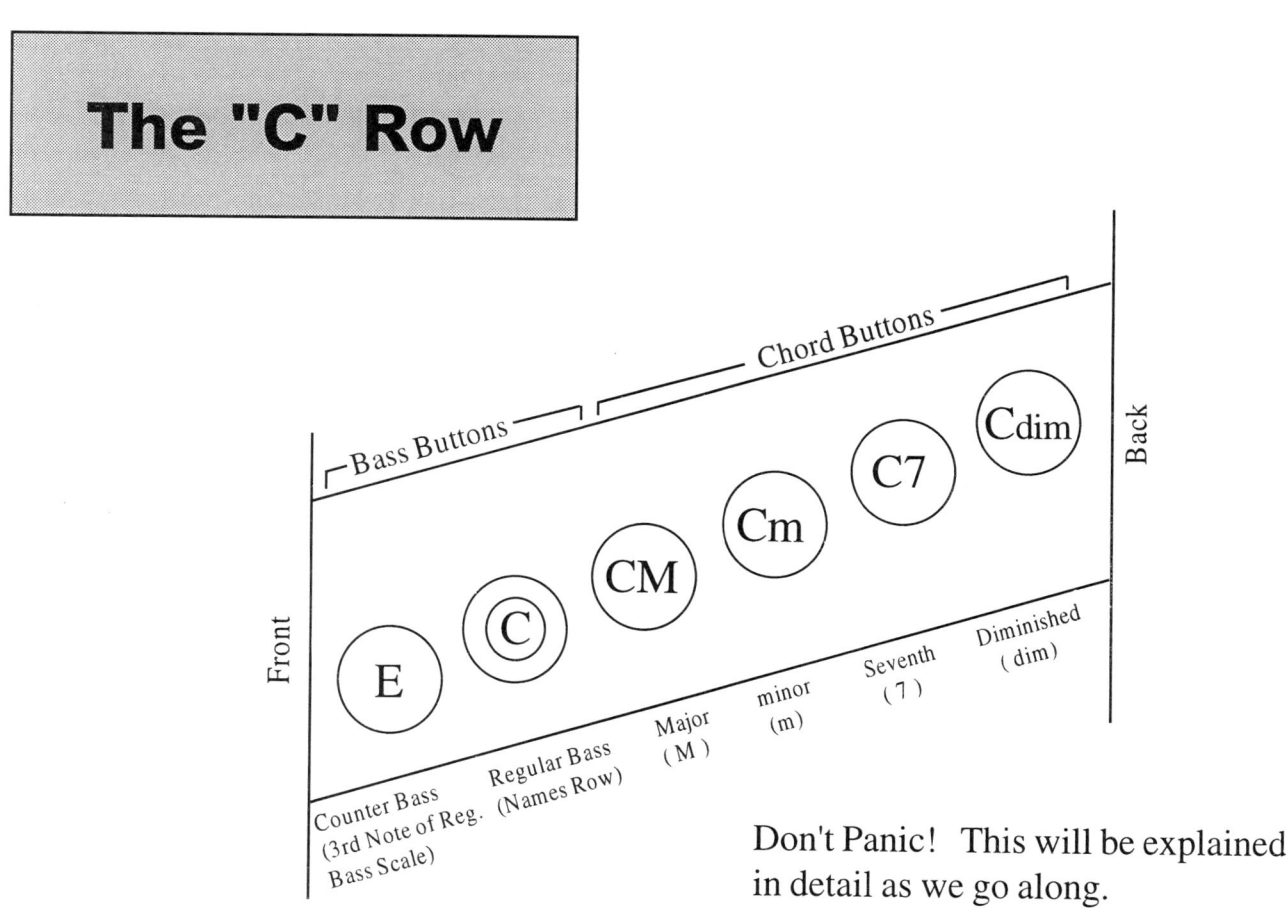

Don't Panic! This will be explained in detail as we go along.

Left-Hand Buttons

𝄢 Bass Clef

In the illustration of the left hand buttons the shaded buttons are the Root Bass Notes that name each diagonal row of 6 buttons.

Remember: The "C" Bass Note is just below the middle of the accordion and is found by feeling for the dip or Jewel.

In each of these 3 rows all buttons are named. All the others are in the same order: M, m, 7, dim, etc.

Some students find it helpful to sit in front of a mirror at first.

Right Hand Finger Numbers

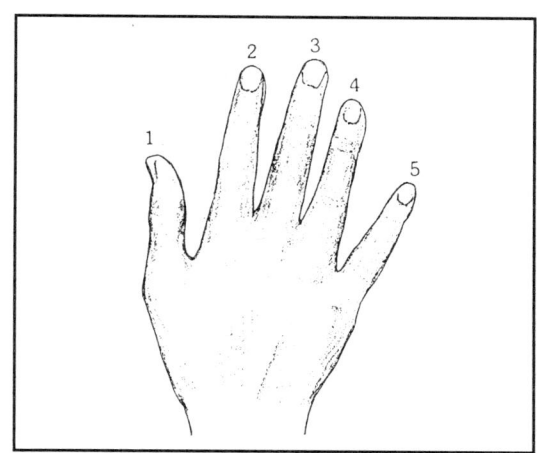

Treble Clef Notes
Right Hand

A B C D E F G A B C D E F G A B

Left Hand Finger Numbers

All chords are considered Major (M) unless notated otherwise.
* Example:
C   = C Major
Cm   = C minor
C7   = C seventh
Cdim = C diminished
Note: some books use a "d" to indicate a diminished chord.
Cd = C diminished

Left Hand - Bass Notes   Left Hand - Chords

C D E F G A B C | D E F G A B C D

Bass Notation   Chord Notation
(Below Middle Line of Staff)   (Middle Line of Staff and Above)

Right-Hand Keyboard

Treble Clef

Position of the Notes

The musical alphabet has only seven notes - A, B, C, D, E, F, G - and then it starts over again

A - is to the left of the <u>3rd</u> black key

B - is to the right of the <u>3</u> black keys

C - is to the left of the <u>2</u> black keys

D - is between the <u>2</u> black keys

E - is to the right of the <u>2</u> black keys

F - is to the left of the <u>3</u> black keys

G - is to the right of the first of the <u>3</u> black keys

Keyboard of 120 Bass Accordion

Lowest-Sounding Notes Are at the Top of Accordion

White keys are the natural notes. Study the layout of these in respect to the sets of two black keys and three black keys.

Black keys are the sharps (♯) and flats (♭). This will be explained in detail as needed.

Highest-Sounding Notes Are at the Bottom of Accordion

FINGERING AND NOTATION GUIDE FOR BOTH HANDS

Learning the "C's"

Right Hand

Count 1 2 3   Use 1st finger

"C" is to the left of the two black keys. The note shown above is a dotted quarter note (𝅗𝅥.) which is held for 3 counts. Hold it down and count out loud.

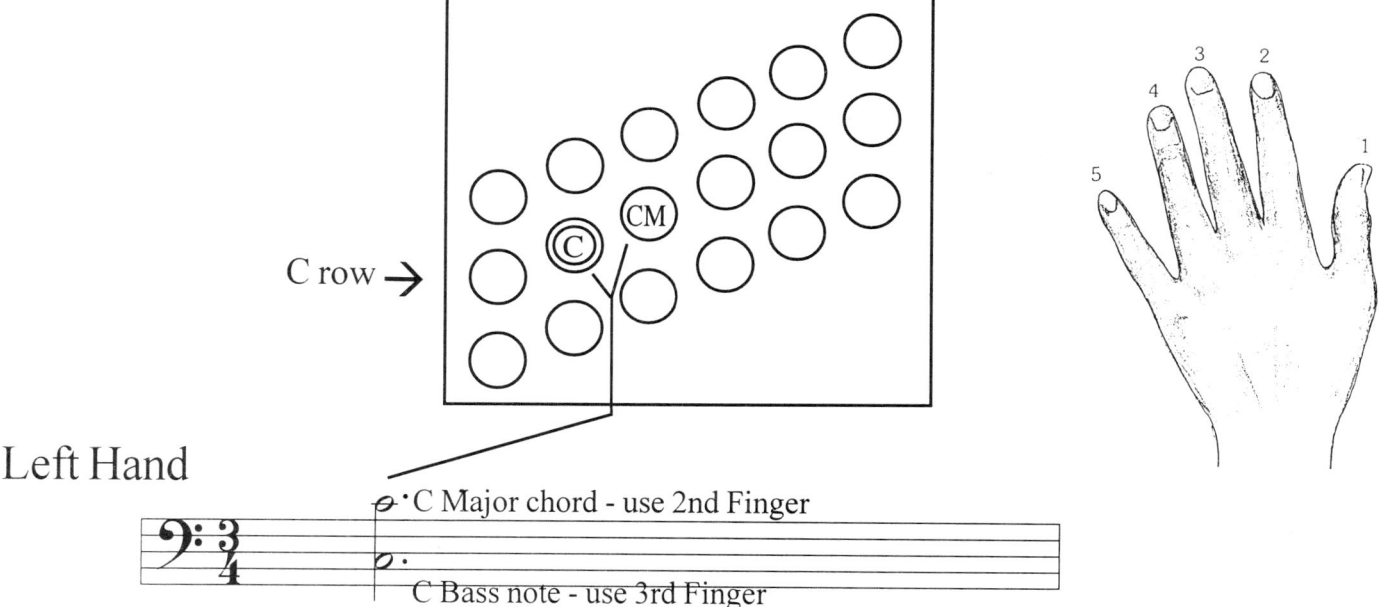

C row →

Left Hand

C Major chord - use 2nd Finger
C Bass note - use 3rd Finger

"C" Bass Note and "C" Major chord. Hold both buttons down (as shown above) and count out loud.

Note:
Fingers should be curved as if holding a ball. Use the tips of the fingers to press the keys.

Putting all the "C's" Together

Remember: (𝅗𝅥.) dotted half note = 3 counts (𝅗𝅥) half note = 2 counts

(♩) quarter note = 1 count   (-) whole measure rest = 3 counts

out = open bellows slowly & steadily
in = close bellows slowly & steadily
* see pages 16 & 26 for more about the bellows

FINGERING AND NOTATION GUIDE FOR BOTH HANDS

Adding the "G's"

Right Hand

use the 5th finger

"G" is to the right of the 1st of the 3 black keys. Again, hold it down and count.

"C" Row →

Left Hand

G major chord   use 2nd finger

G bass note   use 3rd finger

The "G Row" is the next row Above the "C Row". As before, press the G Bass note and G Major chord buttons together, and count.

Proper Use of the Bellows

Open and close the bellows evenly to provide the air to play thje notes – open from the top (like a fan) going in and out about the same distance. Never force the bellows closed – use the air release button which is near the top next to the bass hand strap. Pull a little harder than pushing so that you will not run out of air too soon as you close the bellows.

Mixing the C's and the G's

FINGERING AND NOTATION GUIDE FOR BOTH HANDS

Adding D, E, and F

Right Hand

Adding the F Bass and Chord

"C" Row →

Left Hand

The "F Row" is the next row <u>Below</u> the "C Row". Try to memorize the placement of the Bass Notes and Chords (As shown above) for F, C, and G.

17

The Tie

A tie is a curved line that connects two notes of the same pitch. When a tie occurs, play as one note totaling the value of both.

Put it all Together

Bass and Chord Rhythm Drill

Shown below are examples of the most used left hand patterns. Count out loud and practice these exercises regularly until they are even and smooth. Other patterns will be shown as needed.

Three Counts per Measure

Four Counts per Measure

Two Counts per Measure

Oom-Pah-Pah Waltz

Do not hold bass and chord buttons. Play them short.

Everybody Has Their Ups and Downs

Practice and count evenly   1 - 2 - 3

Bass Chord Chord – Remember to play short.

FINGERING AND NOTATION GUIDE FOR BOTH HANDS

The first 5 note pattern you learned C D E F G is called the "C" hand position.
                                       1 2 3 4 5

Shown below is the New "G" hand position. It adds 4 new notes.

Right Hand
G - position

When playing in different keys the left hand starting position will change. In the example below the left hand will consider the "G" row as the <u>Home Row</u> with the "C" row <u>Below</u> and the new "D" row <u>Above</u>.

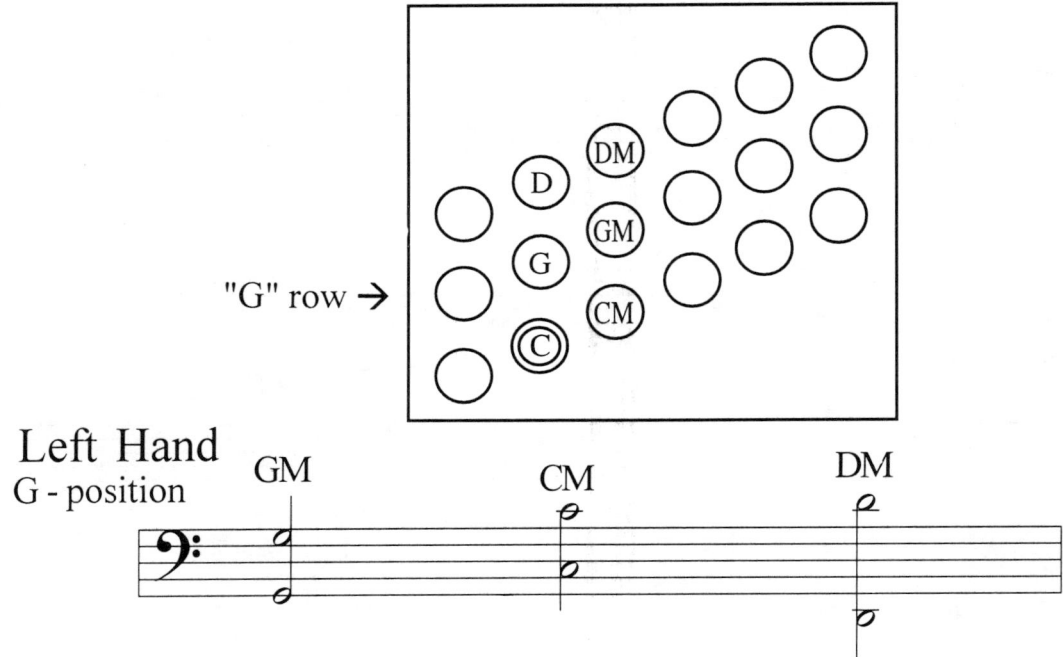

"G" row →

Left Hand
G - position

22

Déja Vu in G

This song is the same tune as you played before in the "C" position. This time it is played in the "G" position and utilizes the new right hand notes as well as the new left hand "D" bass and chord. Use the fingering shown above the notes.

Repeat Sign

Repeat signs look like this: **When they occur, repeat the music found between the signs.**

D.C. al Fine

This instruction which is found at the bottom of the page means to: Go back to the beginning and play down to the word "Fine," which means "the end."

This song uses 6 notes. The fingering shown will give you some idea of "Common Sense" fingering.   *D.C. al Fine*

24

In the example below the eighth notes receive 1/2 count each. (2 played in one count) Count out loud. As shown, the numbers will be the same for the 1st half of every count and "&" will be used for the 2nd half.

NEW BELLOWS HINT - Never change the direction of the bellows in the middle of a note as this will break the sound. There are two reeds for each note - one sounds when opening and another when closing the bellows.

Minuet

Handel

Ode to Joy

Beethoven

The Slur

A slur is a curved line connecting one or more notes of a different pitch. When a slur occurs, hold each note until the next note is played. Do not lift off before the next note.

Shown below is a new one-octave (8 notes) higher "C" hand position. This position adds 3 new notes — E, F, G. Compare the sound of these two positions.

Three New Right Hand Notes

Gavotte

Praetorius

* – Cross 2nd finger over

Alternating the Bass Notes

Alternating between the bass note that names the chord and the bass note from the next row above helps to make the accompaniment part sound much better. Either the regular or the alternate bass note may be played first. Ex: C bass (c-row), C chord, G bass, (from row above C), the C chord again. The movements are the same no matter which row you are on. These will be referred to as "Bass", "Chord", and "Alternate"

IN 4/4 TIME, PLAY

Bass - Chord
Alternate - Chord

or

Alternate - Chord
Bass - Chord

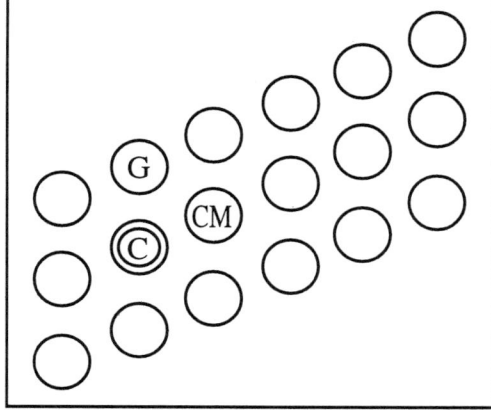

IN 3/4 TIME, PLAY

Bass - Chord - Chord
Alternate - Chord - Chord

or

Alternate - Chord - Chord
Bass - Chord - Chord

Don't Forget: For single <u>bass</u> buttons and <u>alternate</u> buttons use the 3rd finger — for chord buttons use the 2nd finger.

31

The Triplet
A triplet is a group of three notes played in the time of two notes of the same kind.

Slurs (sometimes called phrases) are like singing. A vocalist will take a breath between phrases. The accordionist will change bellow direction upon starting a phrase.

CHROMATICS

♯ - SHARPS,   ♭ - FLATS,   and   ♮ - NATURALS

So far you have used only "Natural" Notes (all white keys), but what about the black ones? They provide tones that are half-steps above and below the white keys that they are adjacent to. There is a whole-step between white keys with two exceptions. It is only a half-step from B to C and E to F, these are the places on the keyboard where there are no black keys between the white keys. See the illustrations below.

Whole-steps

Half-steps

SHARPS

A sharp (♯) placed before a note *raises* its pitch by a half step. A black key has two names possible. Below the notes are named as sharps.

FLATS

A flat (♭) placed before a note *lowers* its pitch by a half step. Below, the same black keys as before are shown and named as flats.

NATURALS

A natural (♮) placed before a note *cancels* a previous sharp or flat. See the explanation below.

Rule: When a note is changed by an accidental (♯, ♭, or ♮), the accidental remains in effect for *the entire measure* unless it is cancelled by another ♯, ♭, or ♮.

Key Signatures

The key signature will appear at the beginning of a piece. It will show whether there are flats (or sharps) in a song. If a flat appears, all notes of that pitch are flatted unless cancelled by a natural sign (♮).

Shown below are the 1-octave fingerings and the three main chords in each key used in this book.

Key of C
No Sharps or Flats

Key of G
One sharp
(F♯)

Key of F
One Flat
(B♭)

Key of D
Two Sharps
(F♯ & C♯)

Key of B♭
Two Flats
(B♭ & E♭)

35

Sustained Bass Notes

In the following solo — hold the bass note for 3 full beats and play the quarter-note chords on beats two and three.

Lullaby

This sign is called a fermata. It means to hold the note extra long.

Introducing the Minor Chords

The minor (m) chords are next to the major (M) chords and are played with the same fingering. Remember the single bass notes are played with the 3rd finger and the minor chords will be played with the 2nd finger. The left hand, when using minor chords, works the same in every other respect including alternating the bass notes as shown below.

IN 4/4 TIME, PLAY		**IN 3/4 TIME, PLAY**
Bass - Chord Alternate - Chord or Alternate - Chord Bass - Chord	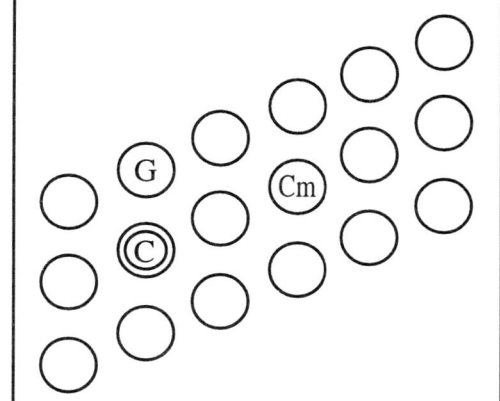	Bass - Chord - Chord Alternate - Chord - Chord or Alternate - Chord - Chord Bass - Chord - Chord

Relative Minor Keys

Each major key has a relative minor key that shares the same Key Signature. The minor key starts on the 6th note of the major scale. The major key signatures that are used in this book are shown below with their relative minor keys. If you are not sure about the key you are in you can usually tell by the name of the last melody note or final chord.

Hungarian Dance #4

Key of A Minor　　　　　　　　　　　　　　　　　　　　　　　　Brahms

Introducing the 7th Chords

The 7th chords (7) are next to the minor (m) chords and are played with the same fingering. The alternating bass notes work the same with the Major (M), minor (m), and the 7th (7) chords. Single bass notes are played with the 3rd finger and the chords are played with the 2nd finger.

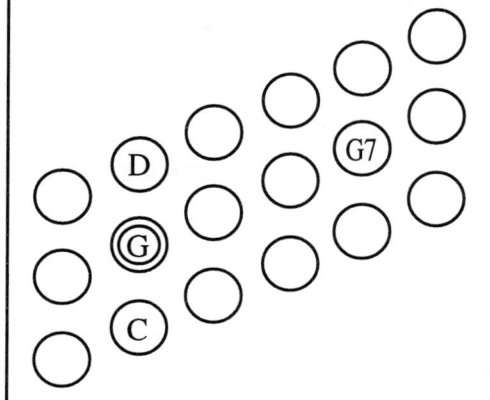

IN 4/4 TIME, PLAY

Bass - Chord
Alternate - Chord

or

Alternate - Chord
Bass - Chord

IN 3/4 TIME, PLAY

Bass - Chord - Chord
Alternate - Chord - Chord

or

Alternate - Chord - Chord
Bass - Chord - Chord

G7

Bass   (7)   Alt.   (7)   Alt.   (7)   Bass   (7)

G7

Bass (7) (7)   Alt. (7) (7)   Alt. (7) (7)   Bass (7) (7)

The God of Abraham Praise

Key of G Minor (B♭ & E♭)　　　　　　　　　　　　　　　　　　　　　　　Hebrew

* Thumb (1) under.

Skaters Waltz

Key of C
This tune demonstrates
the use of the minor (m) chord

Sur le Pont d'Avignon

This tune demonstrates the
use of the 7th chord
Key of G

French

Wandering

Key of G Minor (B♭ & E♭)

Neil Griffin

The Bells of St. Marys

Sixteenth Notes

A sixteenth note looks like this

Several sixteenth notes together look like this or

A sixteenth rest looks like this: It takes 2 sixteenth notes to equal 1 eighth note, or 4 sixteenth notes to equal 1 quarter note.

Eighth Rest

An eighth rest receives the same time value as an eighth note.

Polka, Polka

Neil Griffin

D.C. al Fine

Are You From Dixie

Key of C

Grace Notes

Grace notes are used in Cajun tunes quite a bit. The time is very short and is actually "robbed" from the note it is attached to. The use of grace notes gives the impression that you are "sliding" into the note....

Lake Charles Waltz

Cajun

Key of G

When Johnny Comes Marching Home

Come Back to Sorrento

* Ritard = slow down gradually

Dotted Eighths and Sixteenths
A dotted eighth note followed by a sixteenth note is a common figure in music. Practice the following study until it is felt and understood.

Two Steppin' 'Cross Texas

Key of G

Neil Griffin

Julida Polka

Staccato

When a dot is placed under or over a note (♩) this means to play the note as if it were only half its value followed by a rest equal to half of its value.

Legato

When a dash is placed under or over a note (♩) in the right hand it means to give the note its full value and to connect to the next note with no space in between.

Andante

Key of F

Haydn

Jambalaya

Cajun

Vienna-Style Accordion

Pretty Fair Maid Jig

Peg O' My Heart

63

Rattle the Bottles Reel

Rick's Reel

Introducing the Counter-Bass Notes

The single tone, "Counter-Bass" Buttons add the ability to play scales, runs, and solos in the left hand bass parts.

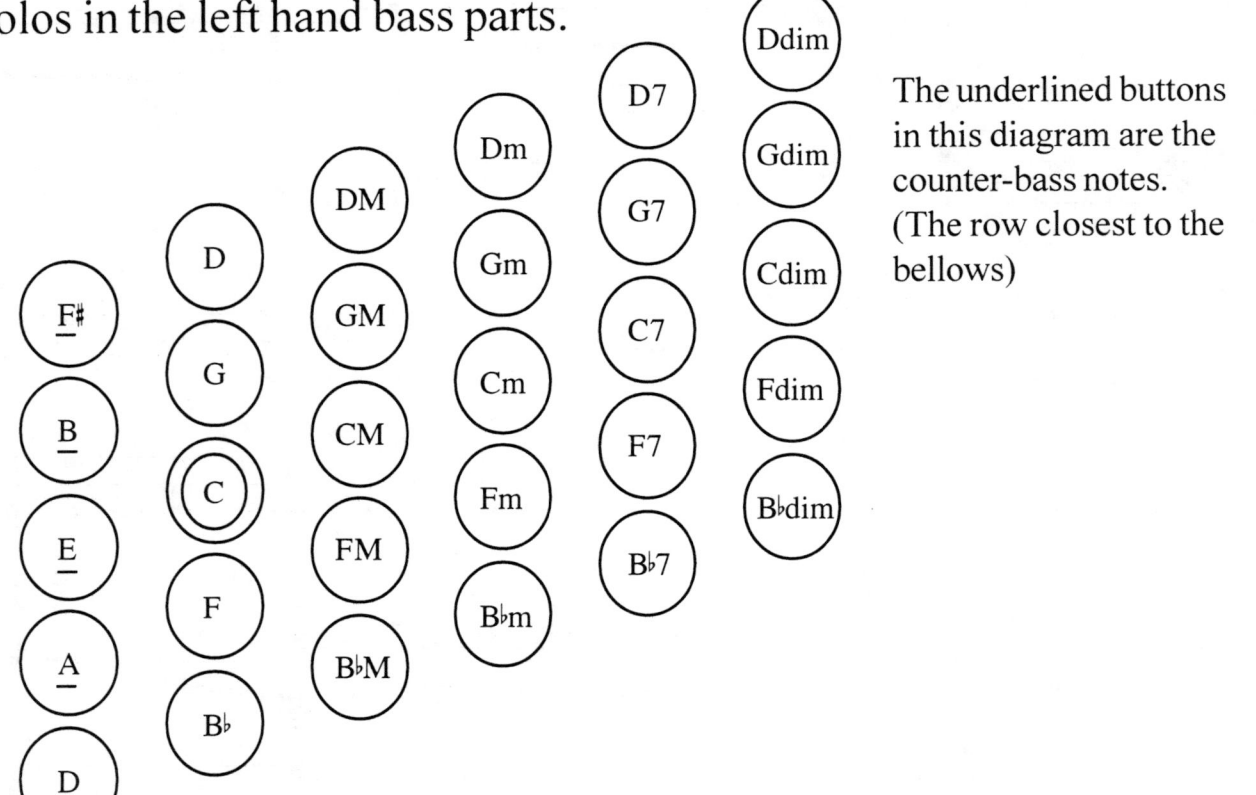

The underlined buttons in this diagram are the counter-bass notes. (The row closest to the bellows)

Shown below is the musical notation for basses and counter-basses from the above diagram. You already know the regular basses - notice that a counter bass is always <u>underlined</u>

In the next several pages we will combine the regular- bass buttons with the counter-bass buttons and chords to produce a better sounding and more interesting left hand part.

Shown below are a few examples of location and notation of counter-basses.

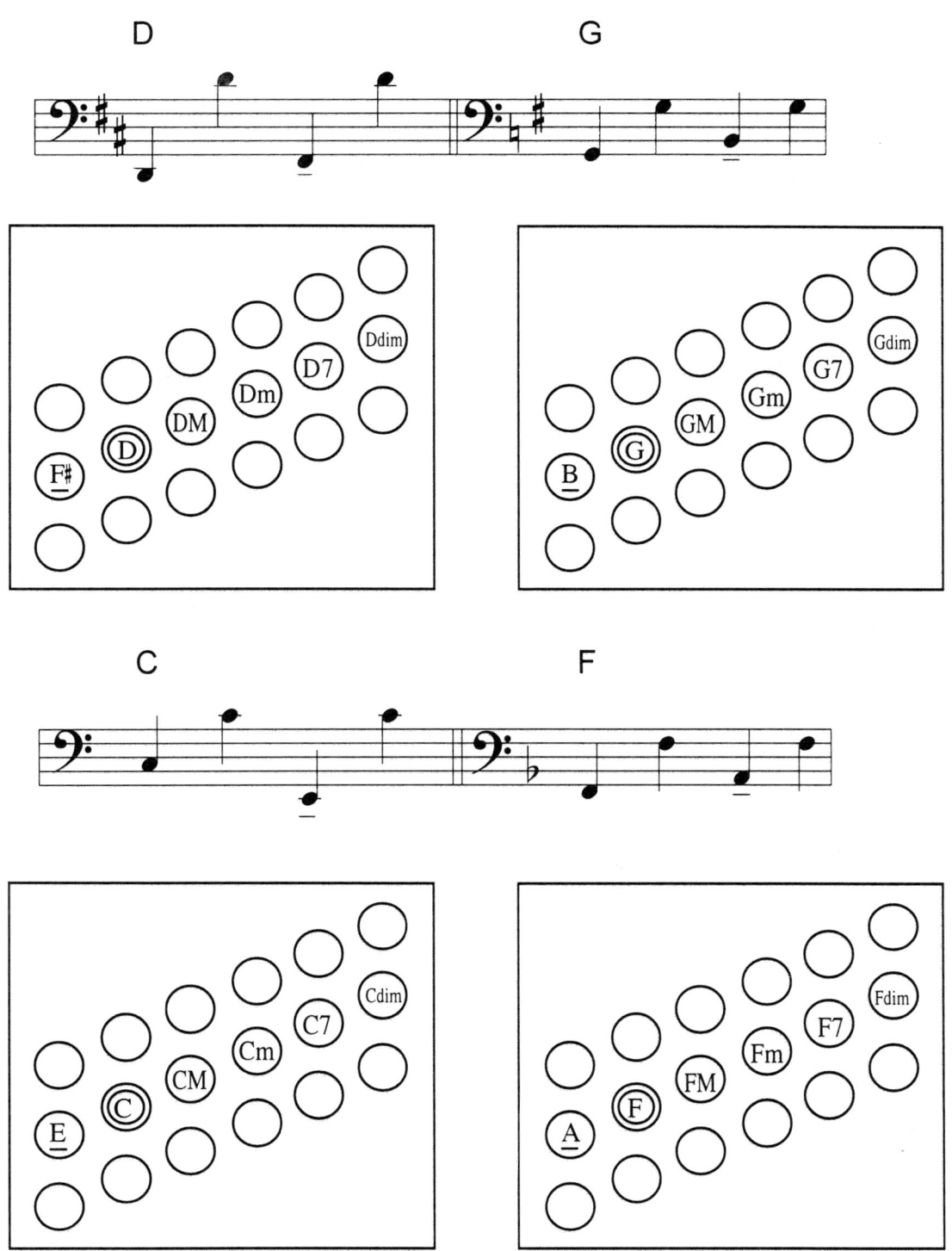

THE LEFT HAND EXERCISES BELOW WILL HELP YOU BEGIN TO SEE SOME OF THE WAYS THAT THE COUNTER-BASS NOTES ARE USED.........

March

Key of C
Handel

Introducing the Diminished Chords

The last row of chord buttons contains the diminished (dim) chords and is found next to the seventh (7) chord row. The diminished chord is a passing or connecting type chord and the alternate bass patterns are not used as with the **M**, **m**, & **7** chords. The bass note is usually the same name and is on the same row as the diminished chord or is the counter-bass from 3 rows above as shown in the examples below.

Ja-da

Key of F

Chinatown

Key of C

Cajun Accordion

I Want a Girl, Just Like the Girl
(That Married Dear Old Dad)

I Love You Truly

Key of C

Smiles

For Me and My Gal

Washington and Lee Swing

Key of C
Intro.

Fascination

El Capitan March

Sweetheart of Sigma Chi

Key of C

Melancholy Baby

Key of D

RIGHT-HAND HARMONY

The use of 3rds (3 notes apart) and 6ths (6 notes apart) provides easy and pleasing harmony sounds in right-hand parts. This is included here to demonstrate how 3rds and 6ths are used.

Mexican Siesta

Key of C

Neil Griffin

BASS AND CHORD BUTTON REVIEW

Left-Hand Buttons

Bass Clef

In the illustration of the left hand buttons the shaded buttons are the Root Bass Notes that name each diagonal row of 6 buttons.

Remember: The "C" Bass Note is just below the middle of the accordion and is found by feeling for the dip or Jewel.

Some students find it helpful to sit in front of a mirror at first.

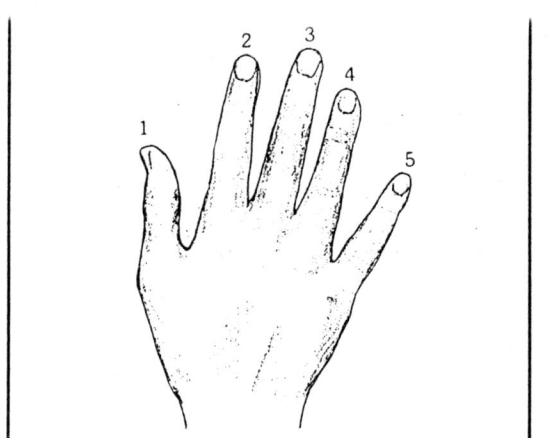

Treble Clef Notes
Right Hand

A B C D E F G A B C D E F G A B

Left Hand Finger Numbers

All chords are considered Major (M) unless notated otherwise.
* Example:
C   = C Major
Cm   = C minor
C7   = C seventh
Cdim = C diminished
Note: some books use a "d" to indicate a diminished chord.
Cd = C diminished

Left Hand - Bass Notes

Left Hand - Chords

C D E F G A B C | D E F G A B C D

Bass Notation
(Below Middle Line of Staff)

Chord Notation
(Middle Line of Staff and Above)